INSIDE HER MIND

by

EMMA MATEO

Table of Contents

CHAPTER 1

The Sixteenth Birthday

The day my dad told my mom that he got his assistant pregnant was unlike any other day I'd ever lived through. My sixteenth birthday had just passed and things were running smoothly in my life up until that point. I was starting to find myself interested in playing piano because I'd signed up to be in a musical elective class.

My friends were all on the same page as me in pretty much every area of life… we all wished we had boyfriends and we all wished we had bigger boobs. My parents seemed to be quite happy and if they weren't, they were fooling everyone who looked their way. They certainly fooled me. My sixteenth birthday dinner wasn't anything too crazy.

My parents took me to a restaurant and let me order whatever I wanted. They handed me my gifts and watched me unwrap them with smiles on their faces. I watched my mom reach across the table to squeeze my dad's hand. Everything was fine… I thought.

A few days later, my dad sat my mother down and told her his assistant was six weeks pregnant with his child. Everything started to crumble and deteriorate from there. His assistant was a 21-year-old college student named Trisha who started working for him three months prior. My dad was the manager of a technology repair company.

He was always very passionate about his work and he was so vocally fulfilled by what he did for a living that it didn't seem peculiar when he started coming home late from work all the time. Instead of begging my mother for forgiveness after he admitted the truth, his confession actually worsened. Evidently he was "in love" with Trisha. He wanted to start a life with her.

He wanted to divorce my mom and marry Trisha so that he could be there for her throughout her pregnancy and be a good father to his soon-to-be newborn. My mother was so stunned that she didn't put up a fight. Her reaction went from being shell shocked and stupefied to total and utter blankness. I never saw her get emotional about the situation the entire time that it was unfolding. I'm sure she kept that part hidden from me behind closed doors.

All I ever saw from my mother was numb and complete expressionlessness. Her eyes were glazed over as if she was dead… I never even saw her shed a tear. My dad knocked on my bedroom door the night he was officially moving out.

"Can I come in, Daffodil?" he asked.

Since my name is Daphne, my dad has always called me Daffodil. He started calling me that when I was a baby and he never stopped. I always loved it when he would call me Daffodil.

"You can come in," I responded.

"I'm sorry you're hurting. I'm sorry about everything. Your mother knows how sorry I am too."

That night, I silently nodded my head with a tight-lipped face because I was unable to openly express what I was thinking or feeling. I stared straight ahead at my bedroom wall, avoiding all eye contact with him. He continued:

"You're sixteen now… you're two years away from heading off to college. I've been here with you for your whole life and I know you know deep down that the right thing for me to do now is to be there for your little brother or sister once they're born… the same exact way I've been here for you."

I remained tight-lipped and didn't move a single bone in my body as he spoke. He went on:

"I'm still your dad, Daffodil. I love you so much. I'm still always going to take care of you. I'm still going to spend as much time with you as I possibly can… I'm just not going to be living under the same roof as you anymore." I nodded my head once again.

Then I looked up at his face for the first time since he'd been standing there in my doorway. I saw tears rolling down his cheeks. I jumped out of my bed and nearly collapsed into his arms, hugging him as tight as I possibly could. I realized at that moment that he was still my dad and that even though I was extraordinarily angry with him, I still loved him. After he left that night, the house didn't feel the same anymore. It felt empty.

Cold. Ghostly. Suddenly the house felt chilly all the time and its constant silence became unbearable. I would sit at the dinner table with my mother and watch her chew her food like a soulless robot. A couple of months after the dust had settled from the whole ordeal and their divorce had been finalized, I remember sitting beside my mom on the sofa and asking her,

"Are you okay?"

"I'm great," she said to me with a weak smile. She leaned over and hugged me. I hugged her back even though the only thought that I could hear bouncing around in my head was about how incredibly fake she was being. She was not feeling great. She was lying to me.

I began to notice that she wasn't sleeping in her own bedroom anymore either. She was always falling asleep in the living room by the fireplace with a glass of wine and a movie playing loudly on the TV. She barely ever entered her bedroom in general. It seemed like she wanted to avoid the intimate spaces she shared with my father by any means necessary. It seemed like she didn't want to be reminded of anything having to do with him.

Then one night my mom peeked her head into my bedroom and asked if I was busy.

"Not busy at all, mom," I responded, "What's up?"

"We're moving!" she announced with a smile on her face.

"We are?" I asked.

"Where?"

"Just a few cities away from here. To Fairview Hills."

"That's... almost about an hour away."

"I know!" she quipped excitedly. I didn't say anything. Because I understood. My dad was able to get a fresh start when he left my mom. He was able to move somewhere new and start over in a fresh environment in a new house with a new woman. My mom was the one left stranded in the middle of all their memories.

I missed my old mom at that moment. The mom I had before my dad left her. The mom she used to be was fun and lighthearted. She was free-spirited and silly. After he left, she suddenly had no personality.

Talking to her was like talking to a wall. Conversations with her were constantly dry and unengaging. Her telling me that we were going to move was the first time I'd seen her get genuinely excited about something for a very

long time. So we moved to Fairview Hills.

CHAPTER 2

Mom

I'm choosing to take my sweet time unpacking the boxes in my new room. My new room is a bit smaller than the one I had before. My mom is able to comfortably lay down on her brand new bed, in her brand new master bedroom, and that is probably the only thing that makes this situation feel more bearable to me.

When I told my friends I was moving, they were bummed out about it with me but they bounced back pretty quickly. According to social media, they don't really seem to be all that phased that I'm gone. My best friends in my old city were Charlotte and Nora.

The three of us would spend time together scrolling through online boutiques and filling our shopping carts with the outfits and shoes we wanted, even though we couldn't actually buy most of it. We'd obsess over the guys on the basketball team and wish they would notice us on the sidelines. We would copy each other's homework and borrow each other's clothes. And we'd all constantly wish we had bigger boobs. We were all on the same page about pretty much everything that matters when you're in high school.

Chilling with them every day before school, during school, and after school just made sense. Not having them around me here in a brand new city feels lonely. And quite frankly, it feels scary. We were the definition of a dynamic trio. Now they are a dynamic duo, posting selfies together every day... and it sort of saddens me to see that they are doing just fine and having just as much fun without me there to be part of things.

My mom works for a company called Solace Solutions. They sell furniture. Beds, dressers, desks, sofas... the works. She is part of the HR department and for years she has been able to do her work from home. Now that we live in Fairview Hills, she's actually much closer to her job's headquarters.

She's able to go into work now instead of doing business remotely… and she wants to be there. The reason she chose for us to move to Fairview Hills in the first place is so that she could be closer to her job's headquarters. I understand it fully. She wants to keep herself busy and she wants to be as distracted as she possibly can. I would too if I were in her shoes.

"How do I look?" she asks me, twirling around in my bedroom doorway.

She is dressed in a business casual outfit and she even has a touch of makeup on.

"You look beautiful, Mom." She enters my room and leans over to kiss my forehead.

"Are you ready for your first day of school? I know that starting at a new school can be nerve-racking."

"I'll be alright," I tell her, smiling.

I'm actually extremely nervous but I don't need her knowing that or focusing on that when she is finally starting to make some pleasant changes for herself.

"Do you need a ride to school?" she asks.

"I'll walk," I respond.

"I'm still not finished getting ready." My mom gives me a quick squeeze and then heads off to work. I can sense a pep in her step. I don't want to say anything that might drag her back down into the darkness she was in before. If my mom is starting to feel better, I'm not going to allow my shitty emotions to stomp on that.

I stare at my reflection in the mirror for a minute. Some girls wish they could make a few minor changes and adjustments with the way they look but I might be the only girl in existence that wishes she could change it all.

I'd make my lips bigger. I'd make my eyelashes longer. I'd make my hair fuller. I'd make myself entirely thinner. For now, I've got to work with what I've got. I open my tube of mascara and begin to apply it in strokes against my lashes.

Going to school every day as a freshman and sophomore wasn't scary because I was going to school with Charlotte and Nora. Starting junior year at a brand new school, totally alone is not going to be easy for me. I can feel the nerves creeping in, taking over my entire body but I try to push them down and ignore them as much as I can.

CHAPTER 3

Laughing Sort of Obnoxiously

The high school campus is only a seven-minute walk from the new house that my mom and I live in. As soon as I start walking up the steps to the front entrance, my heart begins to race. I walk into the front office and ask the receptionist for a copy of my class schedule. The first bell doesn't ring for another few minutes. I pull out my phone to give my dad a call.

The night he moved out he told me he'd try his best to still spend as much time with me as possible. In reality, that didn't necessarily happen. I can count the number of times he stopped by on one hand. His visits were mostly based upon the fact that he'd forgotten something he needed from the garage. Now that I live nearly an hour away from him, I'm questioning how often I'll see him moving forward.

The phone rings several times as I wait for him to answer. Just as I'm about to end the call, I hear my dad's voice on the other end of the line.

"Hey, Daffodil! How are you, dear?"

"Hey, Dad. I was just calling you because today's my first--" I hear the loud sound of something clattering against the floor on his end.

"Hold on one second, Daffodil," my dad tells me. Through the muffled phone I can hear him say,

"Trisha! You aren't supposed to be carrying anything heavy. Let me handle that!" Trisha says something back to him but I can't clearly hear her words.

"Daffodil?" my dad asks into the phone.

"Yeah."

"I have to go but I'll call you back as soon as I can." He hangs up before either of us say goodbye.

I tuck my phone into my pocket and start walking towards my first classroom of the day. No one talks to me. No one introduces themselves to me. In fact, no one really notices me at all. Everyone is sort of cliqued up already within their respective friend groups. As the day progresses I can tell that social circles have already been formed within this high school. No one is even paying attention to the fact that I'm here as the "new girl".

I feel truly… invisible. I see a group of girls that remind me of Charlotte, Nora, and myself. They are casually hanging out, laughing sort of obnoxiously. Showing each other things on their phones. If I was more self-assured and confident, I would approach them. I'd walk up to them and say,

"Hey… my name is Daphne. It's my first day here." But something holds me back. I imagine the looks on their faces staring back at me. I imagine them filled with irritation that I'm interfering with their comfortable conversation. When the school day is over I quietly retreat from my last class of the day and head for the main exit.

My dad never called me back and a huge part of me feels tempted to call my mom and tell her how shitty my first day of school went. A bigger part of me knows not to do that though. I don't want to tell my mom anything that might make her feel badly right now. I walk along the sidewalk staring at the ground in front of me, deliberately avoiding each crack in the cement.

"Step on a crack, break your mother's back?" a voice says behind me.

I turn around and see a girl standing there. She has stick straight black hair framing her face. She's wearing all black as well, even though the weather is a bit warm outside. Black jeans, a black tank top, a black sweater, and black high top sneakers. She crosses her arms and I notice that her fingernails are painted black also.

"Uh… what?" I ask her. Her eyes are piercing. It's hard to look away. I feel like I'm stuck there on the sidewalk, facing her. Frozen.

"I was walking behind you and I saw you skipping every crack. Is that like… an OCD thing?" "Um… I don't think so."

"So a superstitious thing then? Are you into that stuff?"

I meekly shrug my shoulders.

"Well, I am," she says, approaching me.

"I'm Darlene." She holds her hand out to me and I reach my hand out to hers in order to shake it.

"I'm Daphne."

"Cool. I think we're neighbors," she tells me.

"We are?" I ask.

"That's your house, right?" she asks as she points at the house my mother and I moved into.

"Yeah. As of a couple of weeks ago."

"I thought so. That makes us neighbors."

"Oh… okay."

"How do you like it here so far?" she asks.

I'm surprised that this random girl is sparking conversation with me but at the same time, I'm happy about it also. No one talked to me (or even noticed me) this entire day. It's as if she's the first person in Fairview Hills to see me.

"It's alright," I respond.

"I miss my old town already."

"I bet. In my opinion, it's boring here. If I could disappear from this town, I would."

"And... go where?" I ask.

"Literally, anywhere else," she says rolling her eyes. Then she looks up at me and asks,

"Do you want to hang out or something?"

Being invited to hang out by someone feels sort of surreal after the day I experienced at the high school being completely ignored and overlooked.

"Yeah. Okay… sure," I respond.

She follows me into my house and I ask her if she wants a glass of water or something to drink. She politely declines and we head upstairs to my bedroom.

"You haven't even started unpacking?" she asks, poking around at my boxes.

"I never have the motivation to do it," I tell her, shrugging.

"As long as your essentials are unpacked, it's not really a big deal I guess," she shrugs.

I sit down on the edge of my bed and she sits down on the chair in the corner of my room, near my window.

"Sucks that your room isn't a little bigger," she says to me, looking around.

"I agree. My old room was much bigger and it was easier to put my things where I wanted them."

"So you started at Fairview Hills High School today?" I nod my head yes.

"How was that?"

"It was nothing noteworthy. I didn't meet anybody or anything. Do you go there too?"

"Nope. I don't do traditional school."

"How old are you?" I ask.

"Sixteen."

"Yeah. Me too... What do you do instead of traditional school then?"

"I do my school work from home whenever I feel like doing it. I don't agree with putting youths into forced social environments. I hate adhering to schedules and lifestyle stipulations that were created by a patriarchy of old Caucasian men who don't even consider the challenges of being a teenager. We have so much shit we have to deal with and on top of it all, they expect us to be in class at 7 o'clock every morning? I think not."

"Wow! And your parents are cool with it?"

"They let me do my own thing because they know I can handle myself."

She stares out my bedroom window and proceeds to tell me all about how she also isn't a fan of organized religion, gender norms, societal classism, or the present state of political corruption either.

"Do you have a PicGram account?" I ask.

"Ew. Hell no. I don't even have a phone. I don't do technology," she tells me.

"I prefer to stay off the grid… despite the fact that the current generation of people our age is obsessed with oversharing and posting every insignificant detail about their lives. I'm not impressed by any of that, nor am I drawn to it."

"What are you drawn to?" I ask. I don't tell her this but I personally can't imagine a day without scrolling through PicGram…

"Poetry, for one thing. Ever read Virginia Woolf?"

"Mm… no, I don't think so." She sits up straight in my corner chair and begins to recite a quote:

"'I thought... how unpleasant it is to be locked out; and I thought how it is worse, perhaps, to be locked in…' Virginia Woolf said that. Intense right?"

"Um… yeah. That's cool," I respond. That quote went right over my head.

"So what's your deal?" Darlene asks me, tilting her head to the side.

"What do you mean?"

"What's your story?"

"I don't know that I really have one… Not too long ago, my life was as close to perfect as someone's life could be. My friends were incredible. High school itself felt manageable. My parents were…"

"Yeah?"

"They recently split up… and It's been really fucking hard." My voice gets choked up inside my throat. I can feel emotional pressure between my eyebrows and then suddenly I can feel my eyes welling up with tears.

"I want to hate my dad so badly but no matter how hard I try, I just can't. And my mom is a shell of her former self. I feel like I don't even recognize her anymore… my parents made all the sense in the world to me when they were together but… now that they are apart, they've both suddenly turned into strangers that I just don't know anymore."

I cover my face with my hands but the tears are already rolling down my cheeks. The pent up frustration and pain I'd been feeling all day, (starting in the hallways of my new high school), are all starting to pour out of me at once. Darlene gets up and comes over to sit down beside me. She wraps her arm around my shoulders. I turn towards her, burying my face in the fabric of her charcoal black-colored sweater.

"It's okay," she says to me quietly.

"I'm here for you."

As I hear those words come out of her mouth, I feel the tension of my body begin to relax. I melt there, in her arms, and find that I'm able to breathe normally again. I lean away from her and wipe my sniffling nose with a tissue from my desk. "Is it cool if I come back over tomorrow?" she asks me.

"Yeah," I respond.

"That would be cool."

"Darlene and Daphne," she sings as she stands up to leave.

"Our names low key sound cools together," she says with a laugh. I laugh and say it aloud myself.

"Daphne and Darlene. You're right!"

After she heads out I start unpacking one of my boxes of

clothes.

CHAPTER 4

The Bell

I sit on the curb outside of my high school, waiting for the first bell of the day to ring. It's uncomfortably hot and bright but I'd rather sit out here, where no one can see how much of a loner I am than to be on spectacle as a loner walking through the hallways by myself.

Three minutes before the first bell rings, I stand up and grab my bag to head inside. Right as I'm approaching my first classroom of the day, I see a guy. This really attractive guy.

My heart skips a beat when I lay eyes on him. I haven't gotten this excited over a guy since the first time I saw Zayn Malik. This guy literally looks just like Zayn Malik.

A lot of the same features… he even has a bit of facial hair. He notices me, noticing him. Shit.

I look away quickly and pretend I wasn't looking at him. When I look up at him again, he's already walking away. He probably didn't even see. I bet he probably looked right through me. I sit down in my math class and stare at the book of problems in front of me. At my old school, we were nowhere near learning this subject matter.

This new school is light-years ahead when it comes to academics and I have no clue what's going on around me. Mr. Haroldson is the teacher. He's an older gentleman, probably in his late fifties. He explains every concept super confusingly.

It's frustrating listening to him talk. He says everything so frankly as if he just assumes all of his students are effortlessly grasping everything. He's a trained mathematician with a university degree as well as years of mathematical experience-- yet he expects all of us high school kids to perfectly understand what he's saying on the same level that he does. It seriously grinds my gears.

Watching Mr. Haroldson talk is probably the most frustrating thing I've ever had to deal with. I just want to punch him in the face. I've never been so enraged by an old man. After school ends, I head home. Darlene knocks on my front door and I let her in. We head up the stairs to my bedroom.

"How was your day?" she asks me, sitting down in the chair against the wall near my window.

"I fucking hate my math teacher," I tell her.

"Why?" she asks laughing.

"He's a dumb old man with horrible teaching skills."

"What does he do wrong?"

"Everything. Trust me."

"Don't go to his class anymore then."

"I can't just not go. I still have to go. I just… really hate that guy."

"Is someone putting a gun to your head and making you go?"

"I can't just skip school, Darlene. I want to pass the class."

"I don't understand why it's so important to you, but I guess." I sigh and shrug my shoulders.

"In other news... I saw this guy in the hallway that I'm probably in love with now." "Okay!" she squeals,

"Tell me about him!"

"He's tall. He has really pretty eyes. He has a little bit of a beard too." Darlene rolls her eyes.

"Hmm. He doesn't sound like anything impressive. Just another typical high school boy."

"You haven't even seen him. He's hot."

"I can tell you think he's dreamy. But you should consider dating a college guy. College guys are older and more mature. They know what they want. Not the eighteen-year old ones though. The ones that are like... 21 to 25. They're the winners."

"We're only sixteen. It would be statutory rape for me to be with a college guy that age." Darlene dismissively rolls her eyes and waves her hand at me.

"Nobody cares about that stuff anymore." "Really? What makes you think that?"

"It's just common knowledge. No one cares." She says it so matter-of-factly. I stare at her with a bit of confusion on my face.

"You need to lighten up," she responds.

"I'm going to head out."

She leaves and I watch her walk away from my house through my bedroom window. I wonder how high strung I must have sounded to her.

CHAPTER 5

The School

I wander the halls of my high school at lunchtime, alone, once again. I don't dare enter the cafeteria because I don't want to deal with the feeling that comes from sitting by myself in front of so many people. I leave through the main entrance to spend my lunch break seated on the curb where I usually go when I don't want to feel embarrassed. I see Darlene from afar through the black gates. She waves at me. I jog over to her feeling so beyond grateful to see her familiar face.

"What are you doing here?" I ask, catching my breath.

"What are you doing in there?" she asks.

"It's called school." She laughs and rolls her eyes.

"I know," she responds,

"I was hoping I'd catch you for a sec to talk. To hang out. I'm pretty fucking bored."

"I'm happy you came. My lunch ends in about twenty minutes."

She comes in through the gate opening and sits next to me on "my" curb. We talk for the next twenty minutes about how much I wish I were homeschooled like her. Darlene tells me that I should dye my hair. We talk about how we'd both rather be on a beach somewhere right now. We talk about how much we wish we had our own cars. The bell rings signaling the end of my lunch break. With a deep sigh, I stand to my feet.

"Do you really have to go back to class?" Darlene asks me, crossing her arms.

"I'm so bored today."

"Yeah, unfortunately I do." She groans and rolls her eyes.

"I only have a few classes left," I say, shrugging.

"Whatever," she says, holding out her hand to me, waiting for me to help her up. I grab her hand and pull her up.

"See you later," I tell her walking back inside the dreadful entrance to my high school. Darlene really has no clue how much I'd rather be leaving campus to hang out with her right now. She REALLY has no idea.

The truth of the matter is that I'm behind everyone else in all of my classes because my old school was nowhere near this school's curriculum speed. Therefore, I can't really afford to miss a day of school… I'm still in the process of desperately trying to catch up. If I fall any further behind I think I might end up failing out of my junior year of high school.

I stop at the water fountain in the hallway to fill my water bottle and when I look over to the left of me, I see the guy… the guy who looks just like Zayn Malik! He SMILES AT ME. Am I delusional? Did he really just smile? At me? I pull my water bottle away from the water fountain even though it isn't even close to being filled up and speed walk into the girl's bathroom at the end of the hall. I hide out there until I'm sure that the coast is clear. I know I made a stupid face when he smiled at me because I certainly didn't do the cute, flirtatious, normal thing and smile back. I don't have any recollection of what facial expression I could have made in response to his smile but I'm guessing it wasn't a flattering one. I just know I did something awkward and stupid. I lean against the cold, tile bathroom walls and shut my eyes. Why am I like this? Why am I the way that I am? Normal girls smile back when a guy smiles at them. But no, not me. I run and hide in the bathroom like an idiotic dunce. When the hallways are empty, I head over to my math class.

I sit there in my seat, once again feeling inadequate and confused by the lesson being taught in front of me. It's more frustrating than anything else being the only person in the room who isn't getting it. I don't feel comfortable raising my hand and speaking up on my uncertainty when everyone else around me is understanding it. I could ask Mr. Haroldson to slow the fuck down… but I'd be exposing my own stupidity by doing that.

I walk home after class, kicking a rock along the sidewalk with every step. I see my mom's car in the driveway as I approach my house.

"Daphne!" my mom says smiling, opening the front door for me before I can stick my house key in the lock.

"Hey, Mom!" I respond, just as excitedly. I haven't seen my mother looking so animated in ages.

"I have a surprise for you," she tells me, taking my arm to guide me.

We enter the living room and I see it sitting there. It's a piano! And it's gorgeous. Absolutely stunning. Something I wanted but didn't even realize I wanted.

"I remembered that you had enrolled in an elective music class before, you know, before everything that happened with your father. When you were at your old school. You were starting to show a lot of interest in piano so I just figured, why not!"

I stare at it, dumbfounded in silence for a moment because I am completely overfilled with joy. I turn to my mother and wrap my arms around her tightly.

"Thank you so much, mom," I whisper into her shoulder.

"This means so much to me."

"Do you want to show me a song that you know how to play?" she asks.

"Sure!" I chirp.

"I'll play you everything I can remember!" We sit down beside each other on the piano bench and I start to play the first few notes of Beethoven's "Für Elise... a simple enough song to play, yet it sounds so very complex and sophisticated to the listener's ear.

"I'm happy that you like it," my mom says, turning to me.

"I'm happy that you're happy," I respond to her, with tears welling in my eyes.

I'm not sure what's made my mom flip her switch in such a positive way but I'm happy about it. I've missed her. I don't want to threaten her happiness with a single

complaint about anything negative. I just want her to stay

in this uplifted and jovial mindset.

CHAPTER 6

Home to School

Darlene knocks on my door with a forceful fist after I get home from school the following day.

"Heeey," she sings, as she walks inside.

"Hey," I respond. She follows me upstairs to my room.

"What are you up to?" she asks.

"I'm bored."

"I was just about to FaceTime with Charlotte and Nora. They're my best friends from my old school"

Darlene silently slinks into the chair by my window as I call them. They answer on the third ring and the first thing they squeal in unison is,

"OMG, Daphne!"

"Hey, girls!" I say back, waving at them through the phone camera.

They are moving the phone with so much excitement that I can barely see them!

"How have you both been?" I ask, "I've missed you guys!"

"We miss you too," Charlotte says,

"Things are like, same as ever over here!"

"Things are not the same as ever," Nora chimes in.

"Charlotte is lying, Daphne!"

"What are you talking about?" Charlotte shrieks.

"You made out with Franklin Brushberry! Tell her!" Nora squeals.

"Omg, I forgot to tell you that I made out with Franklin Brushberry," Charlotte says to me laughing.

"It was so crazy! It happened over the weekend! We saw each other at the mall and after we kissed, he bought me a pretzel! It was so unexpected but like, I kind of expected it and it was like, pretty much perfect!"

"Wow," I respond.

"I had no idea you even liked Franklin Brushberry!"

"I mean I didn't! But now it's like, I guess I kind of do!"

Charlotte and Nora burst out laughing as I sit there staring at them through the phone screen. I look up at

Darlene who is staring at me with the most bored and annoyed look in her eyes.

"Nora might be getting a car for her sixteenth in a few months so we can probably come down there to visit you!" Charlotte exclaims.

"Omg, yes!" Nora roars in agreement, "Road trip!"

"That would be awesome," I tell them. I don't want to go into detail describing how lonely and shitty my high school is while they seem to both be very happy right now. I also don't want to mention that it wouldn't really be a "road trip" since I'm only about an hour away from them, if not a little less.

"We'll talk to you later, Daphne," Nora says,

"We're about to binge-watch this new soap opera I discovered! It's called 'A Daring and Beautiful Life'!"

"Okay, guys," I respond,

"Have fun. Talk to you later." They hang up and I set my phone down on my lap.

"Oh thank, God," Darlene groans, "Those bitches have the most annoying voices I think I've ever heard."

"Heesh… those are my old friends from back home."

"Yeah. And the keyword here is 'old'. They're your 'old' friends for a reason. Why would you choose to maintain friendships with stuck-up, entitled brats who don't even care to ask you how you're doing?"

"They do care how I'm doing."

"They never even asked you but... whatever you say, sweetheart."

"They've been there for me for years. They are funny, and sweet, and awesome to be around." Darlene puts her hands up as if to surrender.

"Whoa, I didn't mean to sound fucked up! It's just that... I noticed how easily you and I vibe when we first met each other and it sort of irked me to hear those girls not treating you as awesomely as they should. They didn't even bother to ask you how you're doing... That's all. But I didn't mean to overstep or offend you." I stare down at my phone.

"I'm sorry," Darlene adds.

"I accept your apology."

"I'm really glad we met each other," Darlene says to me, in a serious tone.

"Imagine I hadn't noticed you skipping every crack on the sidewalk." I look up at her and laugh.

"I noticed you have a piano downstairs now and it definitely was not there before," Darlene says to me, twirling her hair between her fingers.

"Yeah! My mom just bought that for me."

"I know a song or two," she says.

"Me too but... I don't know very much." We head downstairs and sit together on the piano bench. We each play a few notes to the songs we know and remember. I teach her a little of what I know and she teaches me a little of what she knows.

"You're a lot better than you think," she says to me as she's getting ready to head out.

"I'll see you tomorrow?"

"Yeah. See you tomorrow." Even after she's gone her words about Charlotte and Nora still sort of linger in my brain. I moved away from them and they never even cared to ask me what's going on with me or if I'm okay… not even once.

CHAPTER 7

Brett Carlisle

I stare at the clock in the hallway of my high school, waiting for the minutes to tick down until I need to walk into my first class of the day. For some reason, this hallway feels more uninviting than ever this morning. I look up and see the Zayn Malik guy staring at me. He's at least twenty feet away from me but I lose all sense of balance and normalcy regardless.

My phone slips out of my hand and hits the floor. As I bend over to pick it up with a trembling hand, I see him start to walk towards me.

"Is your phone okay?" he asks.

"W-what?" I stutter, gripping my phone so tightly that the color from my fingertips is probably gone.

"Did your phone screen crack?" he asks me. I look down at the screen. It's thankfully unsheltered.

"Looks like it's okay," I tell him, showing him while also avoiding eye contact.

"I'm Brett Carlisle."

"Hi… I'm Daphne?" I legit just said my own name as if I was asking him a question. Wow.

"I have a friend who works at the mall at one of those screen repair kiosks," he tells me,

"but it's a good thing your phone is still in mint condition."

"Yeah… the case…" I mumble. My mouth won't work properly. Normal words refuse to spew out of my mouth. I need my lips and my brain to get it together and help make me look like a normal girl. Immediately.

"You're new," he says to me, looking directly into my eyes.

"Yeah. I'm new."

Finally, Words! But the words escaped my lips so quietly that I'm surprised he was able to hear them.

"I transferred here last year so I know the feeling," he tells me.

Once again, my mouth stupidly hangs open as I struggle to think of what to possibly say in response. The horrendously cringe-worthy silence ensues for a minute too long when he finally says,

"See you around." He waves and walks off down the hallway.

I mentally kick myself. How could I be so fucking stupid? That was my chance to start a REAL conversation with him. My chance to spark his interest in me. This moment could have been the start of something new and I utterly butchered it by being a silent, gawking idiot. I walk into Mr. Haroldson's math class feeling completely defeated and disappointed in myself. Brett approached me. He introduced himself to me. That has to mean something… right? Halfway through the class lecture, Mr. Haroldson asks a question and then calls my name out to answer it.

"Daphne?" he asks, staring at me from the whiteboard. I've already humiliated myself enough today and now I have to deal with this too? I stare at the problem he's scribbled on the board and then finally say,

"I'm not sure."

"That's alright," Mr. Haroldson responds, "Has anyone else figured it out?" Another girl in the class raises her hand and announces the answer as if she's a pageant queen on a stage or a news anchor in front of a camera. I sink lower into my seat and wish I could disappear into the floor. More than anything, I wish my body would just evaporate into thin air. I see Darlene sitting on the front steps of my house when I get home from school.

I'm grateful to see her sitting there because I currently need to be distracted from today's failures and embarrassments more than anything else.

"Didya miss me?" she asks in an animated voice with a smile on her face.

"I sure did!" I respond, in an equally animated voice. She can tell I'm being a tad bit sarcastic.

"What's wrong?" she asks.

My slumped shoulders must have given it away that I'm not doing too hot. I unlock the front door and we walk inside the house together. We go into my room and I drop my backpack on the floor.

"I fucked up with the guy I like today… Brett."

"Ugh. That high school loser? You're still concerned about him. I bet he isn't even that cute."

I search his name, Brett Carlisle, on PicGram. I pull up a picture of him from his latest social media post and show it to her.

"Okay… I take it back," Darlene says,

"He's actually delicious."

"I know," I groan.

She follows me to the kitchen where I pull a box of cereal out of the cupboard.

"Hold on, sweetheart, you're not about to eat that are you?" she asks as she gently places a hand over the box.

"Yeah. I'm hungry."

"Carb city. If you are serious about this Brett guy, you have to change your diet. Is this the type of shit you eat on a regular basis?"

"I mean… well, yeah."

"No, no, no. I wish I knew about this sooner." She snatches the box of cereal out of my hand and proceeds to dump it entirely into the trash can.

"You have to start eating fewer carbs, fewer calories, less sugar, less fat… less of… everything. Based on what you showed me, Brett looks like the type of guy who has standards. If you want to meet those standards you have to listen to me on this."

"Okay… what do I eat?"

"Vegetables mostly. Salads or anything that has a lot of greenery. And whenever you drink water, always add a wedge of lemon to it."

"Okay."

"Physically, you'll be where you need to be in no time."

"So I can't eat cereal anymore?"

"No, bitch. You can't. Or bread. Or anything other than what I told you, do you hear me?"

"Yeah… I hear you."

"Good." Darlene squeezes my shoulder and leans over towards me in a comforting way.

"It's not that you're 'fat'," she tells me.

"It's that you're… not exactly very skinny either."

I catch a glimmer of my reflection in the hall mirror and

in that moment, I realize how right she is.

CHAPTER 8

Hills High School

I see my mom in the kitchen when I come downstairs the following morning. She is blending some healthful smoothies for both of us with a pleasant smile on her face.

"How has it been for you working at the headquarters of your job?" I ask her.

"It's been incredible," she tells me, handing me my glass. The dark green-colored smoothie looks far from appealing but I take a sip anyway.

"I'm happy to hear that, Mom."

"How has school been going for you?" I hesitate there for a moment. I could be selfish as ever and list off all the reasons why I hate Fairview Hills High School. Or I could keep it simple and say, "It's going awesome, Mom."

"Good. That's great. Listen, sweetheart. I have something I want to talk to you about."

"Yeah?"

"I met a man at work… his name is Doug. He's really… well, he's just wonderful. I eventually would love for you to meet him, you know, if things continue to grow more serious between him and myself."

"Wow," I say slowly.

"That's exciting, Mom!" Her upbeat demeanor is suddenly making so much more sense now. She leans over to kiss my forehead and heads out for the day. I walk to school and as I'm approaching the gates, I hear Darlene's voice behind me, calling my name. I turn around and see her jogging towards me to catch up to me.

"Hey," I say to her, "Good morning."

"Good morning?" she asks in a mocking tone. "It's never 'good' for anyone to be awake this early." I laugh and shrug.

"It is what it is. High school."

"Can you please skip school today? I'm already bored and it's not even 8 AM."

"I'm in no position to be skipping school right now. I'm excruciatingly far behind."

"And? You have the rest of the year to catch up on whatever shit you need. Today, I need you to come chill with me. We can have a lazy day… just hang out." I look at her and then look towards my school.

"Chilling with me is better than the alternative, right?" she asks.

"Come on. You hate being there!" "Alright. Skipping one day won't hurt."

"Fuck yes!" she exclaims, grabbing my arm.

"Let's dip!" We start walking back in the direction of my house. Part of me feels guilty for ditching school because that's not something I've ever done or been comfortable doing. A bigger part of me is relieved that I'm ditching school. I feel like I have no control over anything in my life when I'm there and the action I'm taking right now makes me feel as though I'm regaining some of my power.

Darlene and I go into my bedroom and I hold up my phone to take a selfie of us together. She instantly slaps my phone out of my hand.

"What the fuck are you doing?" she asks, backing away from me.

"Sorry! I just wanted to take a picture with you to post on PicGram."

"I don't do that shit," she says, defensively. She crosses her arms.

"Alright… my bad. I'm sorry."

"It's fine," she says, taking a deep sigh.

"I shouldn't have gotten so pissy." Darlene starts poking around my bedroom closet. I lay down on my bed and put on some music.

"Why on earth do you own this god-awful dress?" she asks me, swaying a yellow sundress I've owned for years in her hand. I shrug.

"I haven't worn that in a long time."

"I'm glad to hear that. The only redeeming quality this dress has is the fact that it probably does a good job hiding your pudgier areas." I look down at my stomach and immediately loosely cross my arms to cover it up.

"Do you ever borrow your mom's clothes?" she asks.

"I have before but not really," I respond staring at the ceiling for a moment before adding, "My mom is apparently dating a new guy now."

"She is?!" Darlene asks, leaving the closet to come sit next to me.

"Who is this guy?"

"I'm not sure. I haven't met him yet."

"Correct me if I'm wrong but... you don't seem too stoked on the idea of your mother dating."

"I have no problem with it actually. I just..."

"You just what?"

"I don't want her going through what my dad put her through, ever again. She's acting super dreamy and charmed by this new guy. If he turns out to be a snake in the grass, I'm afraid she'll be worse off than she was before. I mean, she was really fucked up after everything that went down with my dad."

"What do you know about this guy?"

"His name is Doug. He works with her. That's pretty much all I know. She said she'll introduce me to him if things continue to get more serious between them."

"And if not?"

"Then… I guess I'll never meet the guy."

"You seem stressed," Darlene says, squeezing my hand.

"I do?" I ask.

"Yeah, I can tell. Let's take the edge off."

"How?" She pulls me by my arm and I follow her downstairs into the kitchen. She starts opening all the cupboards and kitchen cabinets until she finds and pulls out a bottle of liquor.

"A few shots of this should do the trick," she tells me.

"That's my mother's," I respond.

"I know. We'll just replace the exact amount we pour out with water. It'll be fine and she won't even notice."

"I don't think so," I respond.

"Stop being a little bitch, dude. This will help you feel better. You ditched school today so let's at least take advantage of the time and the freedom we have at this moment."

"Fine," I respond, taking the bottle out of her hands.

I open the top and take a giant swig. I cough after swallowing because it tastes so disgusting. I immediately open the fridge door to search for a chaser. The first thing I reach for is orange juice. Once I'm feeling centered again, I go for another giant swig. I sit down on a chair in the kitchen before taking a third giant swig of the bottle.

It takes a few moments to hit me. I'm such a lightweight that I don't need much more for it to fully consume and overtake my body. I feel loopy. I feel giddy. I feel free. Darlene drinks from the bottle before refilling the empty space with water and placing it back on the shelf where she found it. We dance around in my kitchen before making our way up the stairs and toppling onto my bed together.

We lay there swaying our heads and our knees to the music playing from my speaker until I drift to sleep. When I wake up a few hours later, Darlene is gone. I turn over and fall back asleep until morning time.

CHAPTER 9

Darlene

I lean up on my bed feeling extremely hungover. I reach for my phone, trying to ignore how horrible my head feels for a moment. I do a Google search for hangover remedies and find that jogging can help sweat it out. I don't feel like jogging at all or even getting up for that matter, but I stand to my feet and start sifting through my clothing to find my exercise gear. I see my reflection in the mirror and notice how bloated my stomach is. I was never big on fitness but now might be the time to get started if it can help in any way. Darlene was right.

What I've been eating in the past has been all wrong. My body isn't where it should be and it doesn't look how it should look. As I lace up my sneakers, I hear a knock at the front door. I walk downstairs and open the door to see Darlene standing there. She looks me up and down with a confused face.

"What's with the getup?" she asks.

"I'm about to go for a jog," I respond.

"No, no, no, sweetheart," she says, shaking her head.

"You're about to go lay back down."

"I'd feel better if I exercised a bit."

"It's okay to be lazy today. Just chill." She pushes me gently towards my staircase and follows me inside, closing the front door behind herself.

"Were you really running to help your hangover or were you trying to get some exercise in to help you slim down a bit more?"

"Well... both I guess."

"Running today won't magically make you skinny, sweetheart. Just chill today. With me!"

I turn around to walk back up the stairs and sink down into my bed. Darlene sits down beside me and leans up against the headboard of my bed.

"Have you talked to Brett recently?" she asks

"Nope... not since my first and only failed attempt."

"When are you going to talk to him again?"

"I honestly don't know. I sort of froze when he was right there in front of me."

"Are you planning to hook up with him?"

"Hook up? As in... have sex with him?"

"What else would I mean you dork!" she says laughing.

"I've never done that before. So I don't know."

"SHUT UP!" Darlene squeals.

"What?" I ask.

"Shut the fucking front door! You've never had sex?!"

"Um. Well, not yet. Why is that so crazy?"

"I just had no idea you were a virgin!" She pauses for a moment and then quietly says,

"I mean I'm not sure why I'm so surprised actually. I feel like there aren't really any guys chasing you down for that anyway... right?"

Her words cut into me like a searing knife. It's true that no guy has ever attempted to hook up with me before. No guy has even tried to kiss me before. Darlene shrugs and adds, "I'm not going to lie to you, Daphne. I think it's super weird that you're still a virgin."

"I guess the stars haven't aligned for that in my life just yet… or whatever."

"It isn't about stars, sweetheart," she responds almost impudently. I lay there, flat on my bed and stare up at my ceiling. Darlene digs around in one of my drawers and retrieves a nail polish bottle.

"Let me do your nails?" she suggests.

She can probably tell that I'm in a total emo vibe now.

"Sure," I respond, giving her my hand. As she gently starts to paint each nail on my first hand with the shiny black polish she begins to tell me a story about her worst nail salon experience ever.

I can barely hear the words coming out of her mouth because the same thought is continuing to circle through my brain. How unattractive must a teenage girl be to be a virgin with zero sexual conquests?

CHAPTER 10

Mr. Haroldson

I sit in math class staring at the board, covered in nonsensical scribbles. Mr. Haroldson is standing there with his arms crossed, lecturing us without taking a pause. It's easy to tune him out because his voice is deep and low. It fades away into a steady stream of white noise. He hands us back our most recent assignment. Nearly every single answer has been marked for being incorrect. I fold it and stuff it into my binder.

It's not that I'm heavily ashamed to be an academic failure… I just don't want other people to know about it too. The bell rings and I walk out into the hallway, holding my binder tightly to my chest. I wish I could quit school and do something else. Maybe if I keep up with playing the piano, I can pursue music at a professional level or something… That's obviously a pipe dream that I doubt would ever realistically pan out. But it's a nice distracting thought to ponder. I look up and see Brett at the end of the hall with some of the other guys from the basketball team.

He sees me and waves at me. I freeze in my tracks. I should be waving back but instead, I find myself standing there absolutely frozen, the same stupid way I froze before. He leaves the guys he's with and approaches me with a smile on his face.

"Hey," he says,

"Daphne, right?"

"Yeah," I reply, nodding my head.

"How are things?" he asks.

"Good."

"Awesome. Well, this might be coming out of left-field but I was wondering if you'd be down to hang out later?"

"You want to hang out?" I ask, quietly repeating his words back to him.

I'm no longer in disbelief. Now I'm in total panic mode.

"I do! You're new and I feel like someone should take the time to get you acquainted." I take a breath to gather every ounce of confidence I can muster. I respond with,

"I'd like that."

"Cool." He hands me his phone and waits for me to type in my phone number.

"How should I save your contact info?" he asks.

"Pretty New Girl? Or is that too much?" Hearing him refer to me as pretty makes me smile and blush. I wonder if he can notice how flushed my face is.

"I'll text you later tonight," he tells me with a smile. He walks back down the hall towards his friends and I leave through the main entrance feeling excitement at a level I've never felt before. I get home and try to chill out despite the fact that my heart is racing and my nerves are taking over. My phone rings and I see my mom calling.

"Hey, Mom!"

"Hey, Daphne. How was school today?"

"It was amazing!" I respond, excitedly.

"I'm glad to hear that, dear. I was just calling to let you know that I'm staying with Doug tonight. I just didn't want you to worry. I transferred some money into your bank account so you can order dinner to be delivered if you'd like… otherwise, there are leftovers in the fridge."

"Okay, Mom. Thanks."

We end the call and I decide I want to hear from my dad too. I give him a call but he doesn't pick up. I try again because maybe he missed the first call on accident. He doesn't answer my second dial either. I sit there in the kitchen feeling antsy, staring at my phone. Suddenly, a tragic thought crosses my mind. What if Brett never texts me at all? What if he completely ghosts me? What if he only asked for my number to mess with me as a joke? I stare at my phone as the time turns from 3 PM to 4 PM. I go up to my bedroom and lay down with music playing from 4 PM to 5 PM. I open my school binder and start looking over some of my homework assignments from 5 PM to 6 PM. Around 6:30, my phone finally buzzes with a vibration. I lunge for it and see that I have 1 new unread text. It says: Hey, it's Brett I immediately start to text him back but every time I start typing a sentence, I delete it.

Finally, after almost ten gut wrenchingly excruciating moments of trying to compose the perfect response, I send: Hey! What's up? He gets back to me quickly: Nothing, much. Do you want to come over? I reply: Yeah for sure. When? I'm obviously much more comfortable communicating with this guy through a phone screen.

Texting is somehow taking more of the anxiety out of the equation for me. He sends: What's your address? I'll pick you up in 15 I text him my address and then throw my phone onto my bed to jump into the shower. I scrub down every inch of myself with body wash and then quickly blow dry my hair as fast as I can. I start applying my makeup as rapidly as humanly possible and then start digging through my clothes for something acceptable to wear.

I find a simple black tank top and a pair of jeans. After I get dressed, I stare at my reflection. I'm not really pleased with what I see but it will have to do. I look at my phone for the time. It's already been longer than fifteen minutes but that's okay with me because it gives me time to primp. Another fifteen minutes passes and it turns into thirty… then another and it turns into 45 minutes of me sitting there, waiting. My phone buzzes and I see a text from Brett.

Finally, it says: I'm outside, sorry I'm late I head downstairs to meet him in his car with butterflies going crazy in my stomach.

"Hey!" I say greeting him in a voice that's way too loud as I open the car door to climb inside.

"Hey," he replies smiling.

"You look nice."

"Thanks! You too." He turns the music on in his car and drives us to his house.

"My parents are inside but they're cool," he tells me, as he parks.

"That's cool," I respond, trying to stay as composed as possible.

"So this is my house," he says as we walk inside the front door. I follow him as he starts walking upstairs.

"And this is my room," he says, leading me in through his bedroom door. I notice his video game collection and basketball trophies. I also notice the nude poster of Kim Kardashian hanging on his bedroom wall from her 2007 Playboy photoshoot. He has textbooks from school stacked on his desk and headphones dangling off his lamp.

As I look around at his belongings, he pulls my body closer to his and starts kissing me. Instead of freaking out like I normally would, I take it all in stride and pretend that I've done this before. I kiss him back and let him feel me up, right there in the middle of his bedroom. He kisses my neck and then guides me over to his bed. He gently pushes me down and climbs on top of me. He's moving slowly without any force or aggression whatsoever.

The fact that he's moving so slow makes me feel comfortable… like I can breathe easy with him. He unzips my jeans and starts to pull them down.

"Is this okay?" he asks.

"Yeah," I say nodding.

"Are you sure?" he asks me, looking in my eyes.

"I'm sure," I tell him. All I can think about is that if I'm going to finally lose my virginity, this is the guy I want it to be with. What else could be more magical than seeing the most handsome boy in school down the hall and thinking about how I'd never have a chance to even talk to someone like him... and then having that hopeless thought, riddled with insecurity, turn into something like this? He gets on top of me and kisses me once more before putting a condom on. Sex with Brett didn't last very long.

Nor did it feel very good. After the initial pang of pain, I felt from him entering, it began to feel like… nothing. It was almost the same feeling of someone rubbing against my arm. I wasn't sexually stimulated at all. He climbed off of me and tossed the condom into his trash bin before getting dressed in his clothing again. I leaned up to grab my jeans and underwear off the floor.

"Do you need a ride home?" he asks without even looking at me. I look down at my feet on his bedroom floor.

"Yeah."

We get into his car and an eerie feeling comes over my entire body. My virginity is now gone and it happened in a way that was nothing like I envisioned. At all. We drive silently in his car from his house to my house. It feels incredibly awkward. He isn't uttering a word and I can't, for the life of me, think of something to say either.

The feeling I have in the pit of my stomach during this current drive home is a stark contrast to the giddiness and exhilaration I felt during our initial drive to his house, a little less than an hour ago. As we are about to pull up to my house he turns to me and says,

"You're not going to say anything to anyone, right? I just recently got into a relationship with Penelope… I don't know if you know her since you're still pretty new but she's a cheerleader at school. Her connection with the basketball team is pretty heavy."

"Um. Yeah. No, I won't say anything," I mumble.

"Sweet," he responds, squeezing my knee.

"I knew you were cool like that."

He stops in front of my house and I get out of his car. He drives off before I've even make it up my driveway to my front door. My legs start to feel weak as I take each step closer to my house. I get to the front door and put my key in to unlock it. I can barely make it two steps inside before I collapse to my knees, weeping. I shut the door behind me but remain there on the floor, sobbing and sobbing and sobbing.

CHAPTER 11

The Burglar

I wake up the next morning feeling like I just escaped from a terrible dream. I immediately realize that the dream is actually my reality. I lay there in my bed, unable to move. I showered three times since hooking up with Brett but I still feel like I'm disgusting. I hear a rustling noise downstairs and I know it's not my mother because she told me she wouldn't be home until later in the afternoon. It could be a burglar.

I sluggishly stare at my bedroom door feeling completely lethargic. At this moment I don't care if I live or die. If someone is trying to rob my mom's house and they murder me in the process, it's okay with me right now. I hear footsteps climbing the stairs and then I see my bedroom door swing open. It's Darlene. Of course.

"You left your front door unlocked," she says to me, sitting down beside me on my bed.

"Oh… my fault," I quietly respond.

"Why are you so lackadaisical?" she asks me.

"I fucked up."

"How?"

"I fucked."

"What do you mean?"

"I had sex."

"What the fuck?!" she squeals.

"With who?"

"Brett."

"You did not," she scoffs in disbelief.

"Yeah… I did."

"Ewwwww!" she shrieks, throwing a pillow at my face.

"Why would you do that?!" "It just kind of… happened."

"Sex does not just 'kind of' happen, you whore! I'm so shocked right now!" I don't reply.

I just lay there feeling the heaviness of my aching heart as it weighs me down.

"So what happened?" she asks.

"He picked me up and took me to his house… and we kind of just, you know, did it."

"Did he take you to get dinner or anything first?" she asks.

"No… we just went to his house."

"So you fucked him after one day of hanging out?" she questions.

"I mean… yeah, I guess."

"How long were you guys hanging out?"

"Not long... the sex didn't really last long either."

"No high school boys ever last long," she says, rolling her eyes. "Yeah…"

"Ew, Daphne! I didn't think you were such a slut!" she says laughing. I don't laugh.

"I'm just joking," she says, shoving my shoulder, "Lighten up, jeez."

"Can we talk about something else?" I mumble. I open my binder from school and see my last math assignment sitting on the top of the homework pile with a flaming red "F" scribbled on the top of it. Darlene looks over and sees it too.

"Are you going to be able to salvage your final grade in that class?" she asks me.

"At this point, I highly doubt it."

"I have an idea to help you pass that class... If you're willing to be open-minded."

"I'm listening," I say looking at her, "Who is your teacher for that class?"

"Mr. Haroldson… He's the worst. Fuck that guy."

"My suggestion to you is that you seduce Mr. Haroldson. Now that you're not a virgin anymore you should be able to pull it off!"

"Why the hell would I do that?"

"Because A. You'll report him. B. He'll get fired. And C. You'll get an automatic A grade for his class." "Nope. Not happening."

"Why not? You'll dress up super provocatively and get him to stare at your tits. It's as simple as that. Make him want you. When you report him, you can dramatize the fuck out of the situation… say he made you feel like a piece of meat. Describe him as being a low life pervert that doesn't belong in any classroom. You'll get him fired and you'll be doing yourself and every other student a favor. He sounds like a prick anyway."

"Yeah he is, but he's never looked at me like that. Ever. Or any other students for that matter."

"Because you dress like this," Darlene snaps as she picks up one of my t-shirts off the floor.

"If you made any attempt at all to be sexy, you would be."

"It would never work."

"It fucking would. You can claim that you've struggled through his class all semester because he's been objectifying you this entire time. They will give you an A+ for his class."

“I wouldn’t know what to wear.”

“I’ll give you a makeover! Why are you so hesitant when this guy has been an asshole to you this whole time?”

“He hasn’t necessarily been an asshole; I just don’t have an inkling of a clue about what he’s teaching.”

“Same fucking difference. Are you down, bitch?” I stare at her eager face for a moment and then finally nod my head in agreement.

“Yeah. I’m down.”

CHAPTER 12

The Phone

As I wait for Darlene to arrive at my house the following morning, I give my dad a call on the phone. Darlene said she's bringing makeup and clothing over for me to give me an entirely new look. My dad doesn't answer the call so I put my phone down. I'm not surprised or disappointed anymore that he's not answering. I just expect it now. Darlene knocks on the door so I let her in. She dresses me in a mini skirt, an extremely low cut top, a push-up bra, and a pair of black heels. I look like a traditional slut-- the kind you see in movies.

Although the first few steps I take in the heels are wobbly but after I walk back and forth in my room a few times, I'm able to maintain my balance. I sit down and let Darlene start working on my makeup and hair. I usually don't do much to style my hair but she's taking her time going all-out making every single curl bounce with definition. She applies heavy, Smokey makeup around my eyes and Fuschia colored lipstick to my lips. When I look at my reflection in the mirror, I hardly recognize who I see staring back at me.

"You have to get to campus a little early," she tells me.

"You need to be alone in the classroom with your teacher for at least a few minutes." I nod my head in agreement as she proudly stands over me like I'm a work of art she's just created.

I arrive at my high school and walk in through the main entrance feeling like a brand new person entirely. I don't feel like my nimble, weak, usual self. I feel the way Darlene probably feels wherever she goes… fearless. Brett sees me and I walk past him as if I didn't notice him at all. Completely ignoring him feels good… It makes me feel powerful.

I walk into Mr. Haroldson's classroom and shut the door behind myself. He's sitting at his desk, staring down at a piece of paper. He doesn't even look up at me until I've fully approached his desk. I cross my arms to squeeze my boobs together. I start a casual conversation with him to make him look up at me.

"If you didn't work here, where would you most likely be right about now?" I ask. He looks up at me and his eyes widen as his mouth slightly falls open. Mr. Haroldson maintains eye contact with me the entire time he stammers up a response of, "Uh, uh probably somewhere in South America…"

For a brief second… a split second… he looks down at my chest. And I catch him doing it. His eyes jolt right back up to mine within mere seconds, but the damage is done. I caught him looking where he shouldn't have. I smirk at him and leave the classroom. I sit through the rest of my classes until it's time for me to return to Mr.

Haroldson's class at the end of the day. All of the other students around me are looking at me. Noticing me. Receiving attention feels different. It's a weird feeling… one I thought I'd be afraid of but it turns out that I'm actually not afraid of it at all. I sit through Mr. Haroldson's class, feeling above it all.

Everything he's teaching will no longer be my problem to worry about. Soon enough...I see him doing everything in his power to entirely avoid looking in my direction. I'll report him with a sensationalized story and he'll be booted out of his position. No more feeling stupid. No more feeling worthless. No more feeling like I hate myself. I leave his classroom when the bell rings and find myself walking straight to the principal's office. One foot in front of the other.

"How can I help you?" the office receptionist asks me. "I need to report something to the principal," I respond coolly and confidently. She gets up to knock on the principal's door and lets him know there is a student waiting to speak to him.

"Send them in," I hear him say through the door.

The receptionist comes back out and points at his office door letting me know I can go inside. As I'm passing her by she says, "I understand you're a new transfer here, but dress codes are meant to be followed, young lady."

I don't even respond to her. I don't have the patience or time. I sit down in front of the principal, Mr. Phillips, who looks extremely uncomfortable after seeing my outfit. He doesn't say anything about it though. "What can I do for you?" he asks.

"I need to report Mr. Haroldson. He's been objectifying me all semester and today he made me feel extremely uncomfortable because he kept staring at my…" I use hand gestures to point out my boobs. "Mr. Haroldson?" he asks with his eyebrows scrunched up.

"That's… extremely odd."

"Well, it's what's going on and I don't feel like his classroom is a safe space for me anymore."

"I'm sorry to hear this. And I'm really surprised to hear this about Mr. Haroldson… we'll have to open up a formal investigation on the matter."

"Whatever. Do whatever you need to do to get rid of him," I say standing up.

I leave Mr. Phillip's office and start walking home. I feel sick to my stomach about what I've just done and I can't seem to wrap my mind around my own actions. I take my heels off as I approach my house and hold them in my hand as I walk barefoot through the grass next to my driveway.

"Hey, girl," Darlene says, running up behind me.

"How did it go?"

"It went," I say to her dryly. We head inside and I sit down in front of the piano my mom bought me.

She sits down beside me.

“What happened?” she asks.

“I did it… exactly what you told me to do.”

“And did anyone tell you that douchebag was going to get fired?” “They said there’s going to be a formal investigation.”

“How long is that going to take?”

“Who knows?” I ask, laying my head down on the piano keys. “What’s wrong?” she asks. “I feel like shit.”

“Why?”

“Because now I feel guilty.”

“Why the fuck, do you feel guilty?”

“Because I lied.”

“Well… he deserves it.”

"I'm not so sure that's true."

"You were agreeing with me yesterday."

"I know. But today is a different day and now I feel like shit."

"You're being a drama queen. Fuck that prick. He had it coming and if you didn't take it into your own hands, no one would have."

"I don't know," I say closing my eyes. I feel numb.

"You did the right thing," she tells me, trying to reassure me. Her words don't make me feel better. Darlene heads out, closing the door behind herself. Leaving me to stew in my thoughts. I take a shower scrubbing all of the makeup off my face.

When I'm dry, I pull a pair of loose fitting pajamas over my body. I go downstairs and try to play a few notes on the piano.

It might have been Darlene's idea but I am the one who actually carried it out. I'm the one who followed through. How fucked up can a person be to do what I've just done?

CHAPTER 13

Showing up to Campus

I'm still sitting there in the same place at the piano when my mother bursts in through the front door. She's pissed. I can feel the heat of her anger and rage emanating in my direction.

"Were you sexually harassed by one of your teachers?!" she screams, running up to me and grabbing me by my shoulders. She embraces me in the warmest and most loving hug I've probably ever felt in my entire life. I burst into tears and start sobbing into her, allowing her hair and the soft cloth of her blouse to soak up my tears. I shake my head "no".

"No?" she asks me, pulling me away from me.

"What's going on? What happened?" I wipe my tears away, unable to open my mouth and speak.

"He didn't do it," I finally whisper. I look down so that I don't have to make eye contact with her. I feel so ashamed that I can't even look at her.

"Why did your school just call me telling me that you showed up to campus wearing an outfit that violated multiple dress codes and that you made an allegation against one of their most ethical and long-lasting teachers?! He's been placed on administrative leave! What the hell is going on?"

I stare at my mother as she yells at me but I have no energy left in my body to fight back or even answer her.

"Did this teacher sexually harass you?" my mother asks me, grabbing my hands.

"They tell me he is a happily married homosexual man… Apparently he's been married to his husband for over a decade!" I feel the weight of the lie on my shoulders begin to crumble on top of me in the most painful way.

"Did he violate you?" my mother asks again, shaking me by my arms.

"No," I whisper, as tears start to roll down my face.

"Then why would you say something like that about your teacher?" she questions me, with a frightened look in her eyes.

"I- I don't know," I stammer. "He was- he was being a jerk!"

"Oh, Daphne!" my mother shrieks, clutching her heart over her chest with her fist. "That is no excuse for you to besmirch someone's name like that!"

"I'm sorry," I whisper through tears.

"I can't even look at you right now! I'm so fucking disappointed," she says to me crossing her arms, "As a matter of fact, I'm actually disturbed…"

She stands there over me as I sit there at the piano. I feel like the lowest piece of shit of all time.

"What made you think something this was okay to do?!"

"Darlene suggested it and I just… I don't know, I guess I just thought it would be an easy way out because I'm failing at school here and I didn't want to tell you because you seem so much happier now and I didn't want to ruin it."

"First of all, you should have come to me. You can always come to me, no matter what, Daphne! You know that! Whether I'm happy or not, you could have come to me! I am your mother for Christ's sake. Second of all, why didn't you tell me you were having a hard time at school? I could have spent more time after work helping you with your assignments, we could have hired you a tutor, I could have sat down with your teachers and asked them to ease up on how hard they grade you considering our family circumstances… there were plenty of other options that we could have explored rather than you taking things into your own braindead hands in such a stupid way. And third of all… who THE FUCK is Darlene?”

“She’s this girl who lives near us… my friend.”

“Why haven’t I ever heard you talk about her? Does she go to your school?”

“No, she’s homeschooled.”

“Wonderful. I would love to hear more about whoever is teaching you how to turn into a scumbag degenerate little girl!” My mom’s words sting.

“Why hasn’t she ever been around here?!” my mother screams.

“She comes over a lot!”

"Why haven't you introduced her to me?" "You're never home when she's here!" "Where does this girl live?"

"I don't know, mom, I've never been to her house!"

"What does she look like?" "I-I don't have a picture of her, she doesn't use social media..." My mom starts to stare at me with fire in her eyes.

"You're lying to me aren't you, Daphne?"

"I'm not lying to you, mom, I swear to you that she hangs out with me here almost every day."

"I'm driving you down to the school TODAY and you're going to retract your maliciously false statement and write a letter of apology to that poor teacher. And you'll probably be expelled for making such a slanderous accusation so we'll have to find a new school for you to transfer to as well!"

I sit there silently. I'm not being quiet to be disrespectful. I'm being quiet because I feel like I'm not even worth having a voice right now.

"I can't deal with this right now," my mom says, sounding completely exasperated. She grabs her phone to dial my dad and then disappears from my line of vision. I can hear her voice fading out from the other room…

"You need to help me with her. She seemed fine before but she is completely out of control."

I go up to my bedroom and start tearing through my things, looking for a sign of Darlene… a trace of her existence that I can use to show my mother. I find

nothing.

I stand up from my knees in front of my bedroom mirror.

I look at my tear-stained face. I stare at my blunt and true

reflection. I see Darlene.